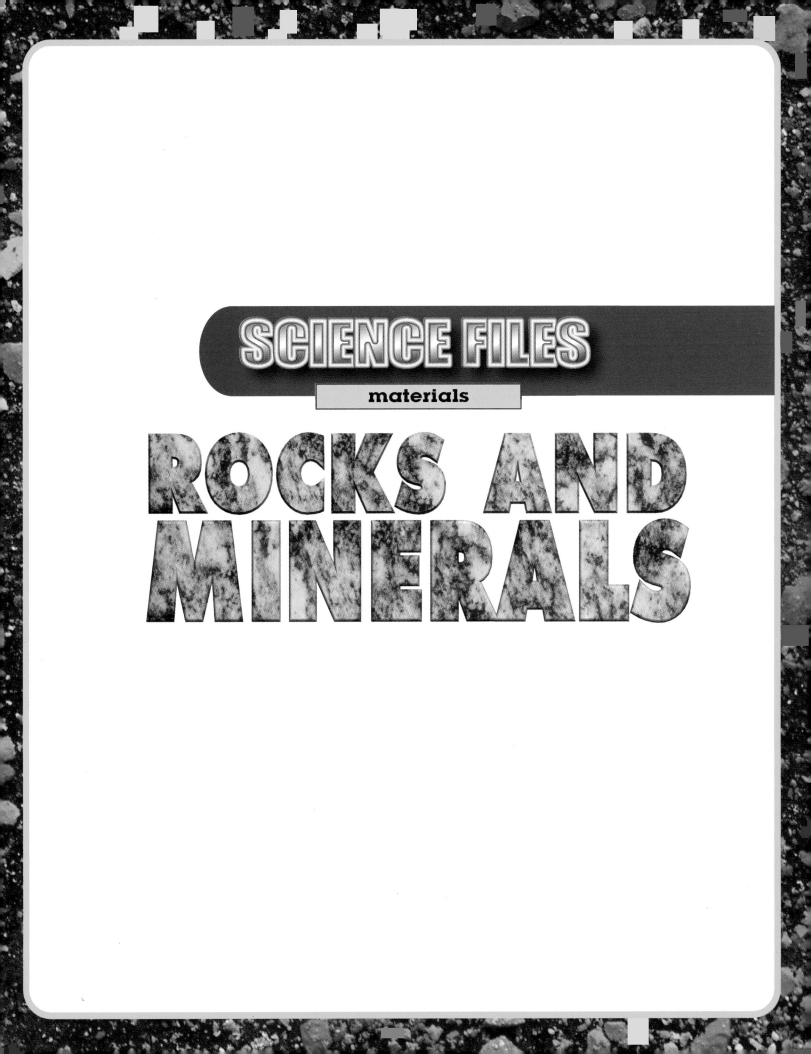

SCIENCE FILES

materials

ROCKS AND MINERALS

Please visit our web site at: www.garethstevens.com
For a free color catalog describing Gareth Stevens Publishing's
list of high-quality books and multimedia programs,
call 1-800-542-2595 or fax your request to (414) 332-3567.

Library of Congress Cataloging-in-Publication Data

Parker, Steve.
    Rocks and minerals / by Steve Parker. — North American ed.
      p. cm. — (Science files. Materials)
    Includes bibliographical references and index.
    Summary: Discusses the differences between rocks and minerals, their formation
  and composition, how they are mined, how they are used now, and how they may be
  used in the future.
    ISBN 0-8368-3085-7 (lib. bdg.)
    1. Rocks—Juvenile literature. 2. Minerals—Juvenile literature. [1. Rocks.
  2. Minerals.] I. Title.
QE432.2.P37   2002
552—dc21   2001054231

This North American edition first published in 2002 by
Gareth Stevens Publishing
A World Almanac Education Group Company
330 West Olive Street, Suite 100
Milwaukee, WI 53212 USA

Original edition © 2001 by David West Children's Books. First published in Great Britain
in 2001 by Heinemann Library, Halley Court, Jordan Hill, Oxford OX2 8EJ, a division of Reed
Educational and Professional Publishing Limited. This U.S. edition © 2002 by Gareth Stevens, Inc.
Additional end matter © 2002 by Gareth Stevens, Inc.

David West Editor: James Pickering
David West Designers: Rob Shone, Fiona Thorne, David West
Picture Research: Carrie Haines
Gareth Stevens Editor: Alan Wachtel
Gareth Stevens Designer and Cover Design: Katherine A. Goedheer

Photo Credits:
Abbreviations: (t) top, (m) middle, (b) bottom, (l) left, (r) right

Mary Evans Picture Library: Cover [m], 6-7b, 15br, 22bl.
Robert Harding Picture Library: J.J. Travel & Photography (15tr); Upperhall Ltd. (14bl); Tony
Whitham (24tr); 29tl.
Ann Ronan Picture Library: British Museum (10bl, 19mr); 27bl.
Scancem: 16tr.
Science Photo Library: Alex Bartel (9tr, 17tl); Martin Bond (12-13t); G. Bradelwis (9bl); Tony
Craddock (12b); Colin Cuthbert (14tr); E.R. Degginger (8t); Eye of Science (20-21t); Vaughan Fleming
(cover [bl], 5bl, 24bl, 25mr, 25 br); Simon Fraser (28bl); Klaus Guldgrandsen (22mr); David Hardy
(10m); James King-Holmes (23br); Chris Knapton (20bl); Krafft (4b); John Mead (6tl); David Nanuck
(16ml, 26-27); ONES, 1986 Distribution SPOT image (11tl); David Parker (11mr); George Roos/Peter
Arnold Inc. (7br); Rosenfeld Images LTD. (21m); François Sauze (22tr); Jerry Schod (6bl); Nancy
Sefton (8l).
The Stock Market: @ 98 Georgina Bowater (12m); @ 98 Lester (cover [br], 5br).
Villeroy & Boch: 18-19t.
Waterford Wedgewood: 19bl.

Printed in the United States of America

1 2 3 4 5 6 7 8 9 06 05 04 03 02

SCIENCE FILES

materials

ROCKS AND MINERALS

Steve Parker

Gareth Stevens Publishing
A WORLD ALMANAC EDUCATION GROUP COMPANY

CONTENTS

Marble rock has lines and swirls.

Intense heat from deep in the Earth melts rock, turning it into the lava that flows from volcanoes.

INTRODUCTION

More than one million years ago, early people chipped rocks to make simple tools such as stone axes and scrapers. More than 20,000 years ago, people ground up minerals from rocks and mixed them with plant and animal matter to make colored paints for beautiful pictures on cave walls. Today, hundreds of kinds of rocks and thousands of types of minerals are used in countless ways — for making everything from brick buildings to computers to diamond rings to strong bones.

We dig up large amounts of rocks and minerals every year. But Earth's supplies are not endless. Such raw materials must be used with great care and recycled whenever possible.

Although a glistening, sparkling diamond is one of the world's most precious items, it is a simple mineral made by natural processes beneath Earth's surface.

ROCK OR MINERAL?

Beneath our feet, the outer layer of Earth is made of hard, tough natural substances called rocks.

TYPES OF ROCKS

There are many kinds of rocks, such as flint, sandstone, limestone, marble, slate, granite, and basalt. Each has its own color, hardness, heaviness, and texture.

Since ancient times, people have shaped or carved rocks to make statues. Each of these giant heads on Easter Island, in the Pacific Ocean, weighs more than a truck.

Amethyst

Chalcedony

Icicle-like mineral deposits are left behind in caves by water dripping from the cave's roof or onto its floor. Stalagmites (left) rise up, while stalactites hang down.

▼ *The minerals below are prized for their colors and patterns. When they are smoothed and polished, they shine and sparkle.*

Agate

Lapis lazuli

Turquoise

Opal

Amber

WHAT ARE MINERALS?

Minerals are made of a combination of the simplest natural substances of all: chemical elements. For example, the mineral calcite, also called calcium carbonate, is made up of one part of the chemical element calcium (Ca), one part of the element carbon (C), and three parts of the element oxygen (O). This is why scientists use the symbol "$CaCO_3$" for calcite.

FACTS FROM THE PAST

Each type of rock has features that make it useful in some way. For example, with careful hammering, flint can be split into thin, sharp-edged pieces. It was therefore one of the first rocks people used to make tools such as scrapers and knives and weapons like arrowheads, spearheads, and daggers.

These arrowheads are 4,000 years old.

WHAT ARE ROCKS MADE OF?

Rocks are made of basic natural substances called minerals. Each rock has its own combination of minerals. Marble, for example, is made mainly of the minerals calcite and dolomite.

THE ROCK CYCLE

Earth's rocks may seem strong enough to last forever. But they do not. Very slowly, they change. They are worn away by the weather, and they are squeezed and melted by huge forces deep within Earth. Gradually, old rocks are destroyed and new ones form. This process is called the rock cycle.

Lava from a volcano may take years to cool down and harden.

Lava (molten rock on the surface) cools and becomes solid, forming igneous rock.

Strong heat near magma changes the magma into a new kind of rock, which is called metamorphic rock.

Magma (underground molten rock)

In warm shallow seas, small, soft creatures build hard mineral skeletons around themselves. These build up into coral reefs.

BREAKING DOWN

Over thousands of years, even the hardest rocks are worn down by the forces of nature. These forces include the hot Sun, freezing ice, rain, snow, glaciers, waves, and winds carrying sand and dust. This process of wearing down is known as erosion.

IDEAS FOR THE FUTURE

When rock becomes very hot — usually 1,830° F (1,000° C) or higher — it melts and becomes liquid. This is why lava oozes or spurts from a volcano. If the flowing lava could be poured into block-shaped molds, it would cool and solidify in the shape of the molds. If the molds were removed — instant building bricks!

MAIN TYPES OF ROCKS

There are three main types of rocks, each made in a different way. Igneous rocks form when molten rock hardens. Metamorphic rocks form when great heat and pressure change one type of rock into a new type. Sedimentary rocks form as pieces of rock settle in layers, known as sediments, then become squeezed and naturally glued together.

Wind, rain, waves, and ice erode (wear down) rocks into small particles.

Particles of rock are blown by the wind and carried by rivers into the sea.

Sedimentary rock forms when particles sink, form layers, and become stuck together.

High pressure far underground turns original rock into new metamorphic rock.

On coasts, waves erode the rocks and create shapes such as arches.

Mud and other mineral particles settle at the mouths of rivers.

BUILDING UP

The forces of nature destroy old rocks, but their mineral particles are not lost. Huge amounts of heat and pressure squash or even melt these tiny pieces. Other minerals work like natural glue to stick them together. The results are huge, hard lumps of new rock — and so the cycle goes on.

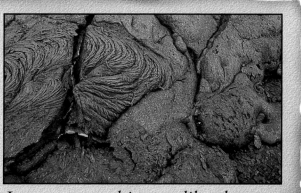

Lava may cool in ropelike shapes.

FINDING USEFUL ROCKS

Rocks are everywhere — bare and exposed on the ground or buried under soil and plants. But not all rocks are rich in minerals or suitable for uses such as building. Special scientists, known as geologists, must search for rocks that are useful.

EYES IN THE SKIES

Geologists begin their search for useful rocks by studying photographs taken by satellites or from high-flying planes. They recognize different types of rocks in the photographs by their various colors and surface features.

Survey satellites, such as SPOT, circle Earth and take pictures of the ground and rocks.

FACTS FROM THE PAST

Throughout recorded history, people have eagerly rushed to places where precious minerals have been discovered — especially gems like diamonds. These "jewel rushes" cause buildings and towns to spring up in places like mountains, deserts, and swamps.

Diamond rush in South Africa, 1895

ROCK SHOCK

You can feel the ground vibrate when a passing truck shakes the rocks in it. Stronger shocks or seismic waves also travel through rock. Their speed and the way they fade in strength and deflect (change direction) indicate the types and layers of rocks under the surface.

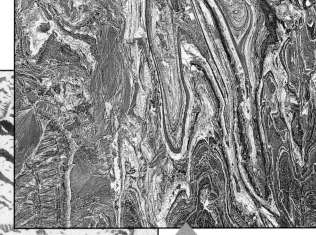

Patterns and colors visible in pictures of the Iranian desert (above) and the mountains of the Himalayas (left) show rocks rich in certain minerals.

TESTS AT THE SITE

When photographs reveal a place with useful rocks, geologists travel to that area for on-site studies. They use small explosions or "thumper" machines to see how shock waves travel through the ground (*see below*). They also drill into the rocks and remove small pieces, or samples, to take back to their laboratories for further tests.

The vibro-truck has a large plate between the wheels, which sends shock waves through the ground to find rocks.

Seismic waves are made by explosives or vibrating machines. Rows of delicate sensors detect them, and a computer shows the results.

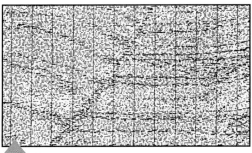

Printout of a seismic survey

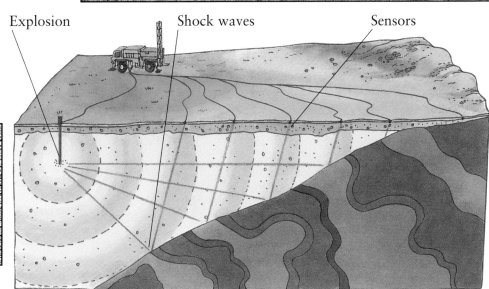

Explosion   Shock waves   Sensors

MINES AND QUARRIES

Mines are places where minerals or mineral-rich rocks are dug out of the ground. Blocks of stone, used to create building materials, come from quarries.

MINES AT THE SURFACE

Where soft, mineral-rich rocks are on or near Earth's surface, they are scraped up by massive excavator machines. Harder rocks are first loosened by blasting with explosives. This is known as strip mining or open-pit mining. The rocks are usually taken away in huge trucks for the next stage, which is separating out the useful minerals.

Some deep mines are big enough to contain railways and trucks. Digging continues until the mine is "worked out" — no longer worth digging through the rocks.

Strip mines destroy the landscape. In many places today, they must be covered with soil and trees.

MINES BELOW GROUND

If the mineral-rich rocks are deep underground, a vertical elevator shaft is drilled or blasted downward. Then tunnels, called galleries, are dug sideways into the rock. The rock is then broken up and taken away. As a gallery is dug lengthwise, it may change direction to follow the mineral-rich band, or seam, of rock.

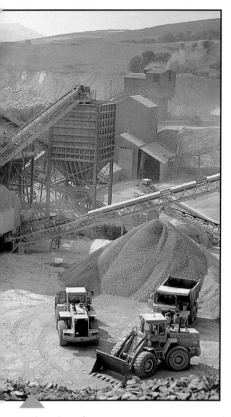

Blocks from quarries used for paving slabs, statues, and buildings are called "dimension" stone. Sand and shingle make up "aggregate" stone.

IDEAS FOR THE FUTURE

In certain places on the seabed, Earth's natural processes have made nodules, or deposits of large amounts of pure minerals. Deep-sea submersible crafts could gather these deposits. This would reduce the mining of rocks on land, which contain less mineral.

Gathering minerals in the deep sea

HOLES, TUNNELS, AND DREDGES

Strip-mine pit

Some mineral-rich rocks are mined from giant holes that connect to elevator shafts leading down to deep tunnels.

Some sediments contain plentiful minerals. They are mined by dredging ships or shore-based excavators.

Bucket-wheel excavator

Underground mine

Shaft   Deep tunnels

Dredging ship   Sediment

BLOCKS AND BRICKS

To make the walls of a house, you could simply pile up pieces of rock. But you could build stronger, more stable, safer walls out of rocks shaped into boxlike blocks or bricks. Bricks are made by mixing clay-rich minerals, forming them into box shapes, and baking them until they are hard.

Rough, gray bricks are used to build inside walls. They are faced (covered) with red bricks.

Colored bricks and tiles can make decorative patterns and designs, as on the Summer Palace in Khosa, Uzbekistan, in Central Asia.

THE BRICKYARD

Special kinds of clay or shale are crushed by machines until they are reduced to a fine clay powder. This powder is mixed with additive and coloring chemicals. When mixed with

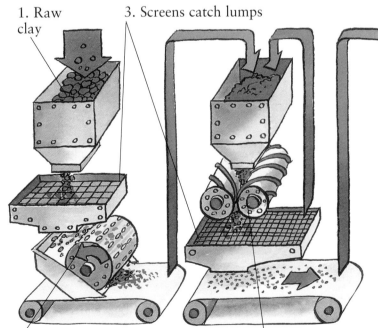

1. Raw clay

3. Screens catch lumps

2. Crushers break the clay into tiny pieces

14

NO CRACKS OR GAPS

Natural rock can be shaped or carved with saws, chisels, and other tools into blocks, round-edged cobblestones, and thinner slabs and tiles. But the rock must not contain any tiny cracks or it could shatter under the weight of more blocks above. Bricks can be mass-produced, without cracks, to the same quality and size so they fit closely, without gaps. They are joined using another mineral product, cement (*see next page*).

Cobblestones ▶

water, the clay powder becomes a thick paste. After air bubbles are removed, the paste is molded into bricks and baked hard in kilns.

Adobe bricks are made from natural mud minerals, simply mixed and baked in the sun. These multistory houses in South Yemen are the world's tallest mud-brick structures.

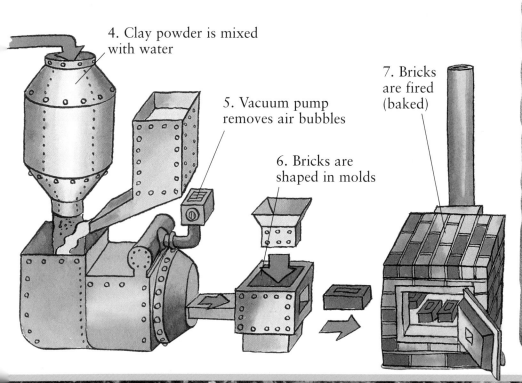

4. Clay powder is mixed with water

5. Vacuum pump removes air bubbles

6. Bricks are shaped in molds

7. Bricks are fired (baked)

FACTS FROM THE PAST

Some of the world's oldest and greatest structures, the Pyramids of Ancient Egypt, were made from natural stone. Groups of people cut, shaped, dragged, and lifted the blocks, each weighing many tons, all by hand.

Pyramid under construction

CEMENT AND CONCRETE

Cement is one of the most important building materials in the world. A very fine, grayish powder made from various rocks and minerals, cement is mixed with sand and water to form a paste, called mortar, which is used to hold bricks together.

Concrete or mortar can be delivered ready-mixed by truck. But once water is added, setting begins and cannot be stopped. The truck's large rotating drum keeps the cement moving to prevent it from setting.

Making cement uses up huge amounts of raw materials and energy. More than one billion tons of cement are made every year.

THE CEMENT WORKS

Raw materials for cement vary, depending on the type being made. It may be made to set very fast or to withstand acids or heat.

The raw materials are dried, mixed, and crushed in grinding mills. The resulting powder is agitated (shaken) and stored.

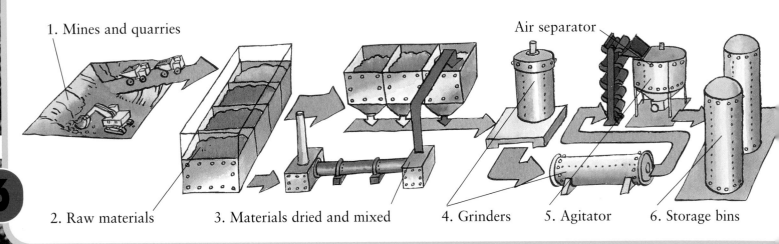

1. Mines and quarries

Air separator

2. Raw materials   3. Materials dried and mixed   4. Grinders   5. Agitator   6. Storage bins

CONCRETE

Cement, water, sand (fine aggregate), and gravel (coarse aggregate) mix to make concrete. Like mortar, this mixture sets hard by chemical action, rather than by drying out. For this reason, concrete can be used for building dams and bridge towers, as well as for many other structures such as tunnels, skyscrapers, floors, roadways, and wall panels.

Concrete is very hard, but it may crack as it bends, so steel rods or frames are put inside it for extra strength. This is reinforced concrete.

IDEAS FOR THE FUTURE

As concrete's strength is improved, architects can plan skyscrapers that are taller and slimmer. In this design (right), a tower has a tapered top that seems to disappear into the sky.

A mile-high tower?

The mix is heated in a kiln to make clinker. Gypsum is added and the final cement is milled to a powder.

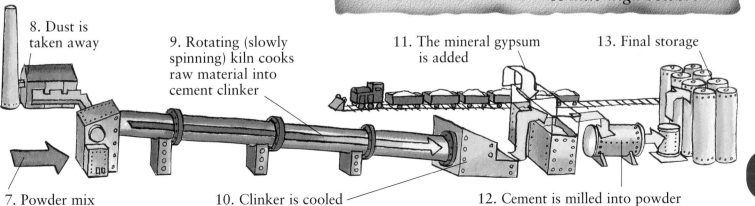

8. Dust is taken away

9. Rotating (slowly spinning) kiln cooks raw material into cement clinker

11. The mineral gypsum is added

13. Final storage

7. Powder mix

10. Clinker is cooled

12. Cement is milled into powder

17

POTTERY AND PORCELAIN

Clays are naturally squishy, fine-grained, earthy substances from the ground. Most contain the minerals silica and alumina. They harden when dry and become even harder if heated in an oven. People have used mineral-rich clay for thousands of years to make jars, vases, cups, bowls, plates, and pots. These items are known as pottery.

THE MAKING OF A MUG

In many ways, making pottery is similar to cooking. The ingredients, including pigments, are mixed together depending on the type of pottery needed. Much of the skill lies in knowing how hot and how long to fire, or "cook," the shaped clay in the kiln.

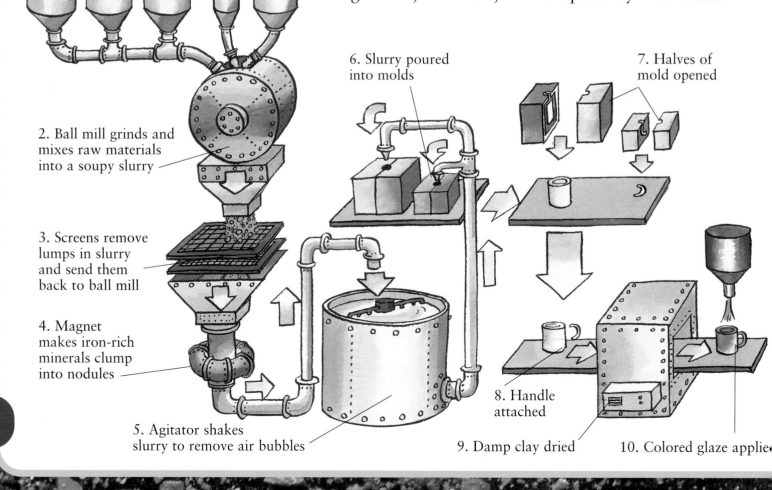

1. Clay, feldspar, flint particles, water, and other raw materials

Water

2. Ball mill grinds and mixes raw materials into a soupy slurry

3. Screens remove lumps in slurry and send them back to ball mill

4. Magnet makes iron-rich minerals clump into nodules

5. Agitator shakes slurry to remove air bubbles

6. Slurry poured into molds

7. Halves of mold opened

8. Handle attached

9. Damp clay dried

10. Colored glaze applied

Today pottery is made on a production line. Here, tableware is stacked, ready to be decorated either with transfers or by printing. After that, a clear glaze is then applied to protect the decoration.

This tea set is made of porcelain. Porcelain is made from kaolin (china clay), which contains the mineral feldspar which is very hard and shiny. Porcelain items are so thin they are translucent (letting light through).

Making items on a potter's wheel has not changed over thousands of years.

11. Mug fired in kiln

SHAPED AND BAKED

Only certain kinds of clays are suitable for pottery. Different clays may be mixed or blended and water added to make them into a paste. Items are shaped on a slowly spinning potter's wheel or in molds. Then they are baked, or fired, in a kiln (oven) to make them hard.

CERAMICS AND COMPOSITES

Clay-rich soils and minerals have many uses, such as making bricks and pots, as shown on previous pages. The general name for objects made from clay is ceramics, but there is much more to them than bricks and pots.

HIGH-TECH CERAMICS

In addition to being used for many everyday purposes, ceramics are also used for making many high-tech items. To make these objects, clays are blended and mixed with various other minerals and substances, then heated to more than 2,730° F (1,500° C) in high-temperature kilns.

Many ceramics, like the white part of this spark plug, are insulators. They do not conduct electricity.

Piles of saucer-shaped ceramic insulators keep high-power cables apart so electricity does not leak between them or into the ground.

Many ceramics can withstand intense heat. These are used as linings in furnaces and kilns and as tiles on space shuttles.

Flexible fibers, like glass fiber, can be bent easily, but they are not very hard. Ceramics are very hard, but if bent, they crack. A ceramic-fiber composite combines the best features of both.

CLAY COMBINATIONS

Ceramic composites are combinations of ceramics and other materials, such as metals, minerals, glass, or carbon fiber. Each type of composite has its own special features. Ceramic-metal composites are incredibly hard, which makes them ideal for bearings and other moving parts in high-speed machines. Ceramic-fiber composites are light but tough, and they resist heat. They are used for fireproof clothing.

Mineral oils can also be made into aramide, a strong fiber used for boat sails and the wings of hang gliders.

IDEAS FOR THE FUTURE

Metal power cables let through most electricity, but waste some. Future composite cables of ceramic and metal may be "superconductors" that let all electricity through, wasting none.

Overhead power cables

MINERAL CRYSTALS

Most minerals occur naturally in the form of crystals. All crystals have flat sides, angled edges, and sharp corners. Minerals in crystal form have many amazing features and uses.

OLD AND NEW

Since ancient times, people have loved the shapes and colors of crystals. In modern science, crystals are used to change electricity into vibrations or light.

A familiar crystal substance is common salt, obtained from rocks or after seawater dries. The crystals are called "grains."

FACTS FROM THE PAST

Scientist Pierre Curie discovered that when electricity is passed through a crystal, it changes shape slightly. Also, when a crystal is squeezed, it produces a tiny pulse of electricity. This is known as the piezoelectric effect.

Pierre Curie (1859-1906)

Crystals are used in liquid crystal displays, also known as the LCDs.

The mineral quartz, a type of silica, forms large, clear crystals. These may be polished into the "crystal balls" that fortune tellers use to predict the future.

Microchips are made from silicon, found in the mineral quartz. Crystals of quartz are made in laboratories and sliced into thin wafers. Each wafer is coated to be sensitive to ultraviolet light, which is shined through a stencil and burns the shapes of the chip's tiny electronic circuits onto the wafer. Acids wash away the coating to leave only the circuits.

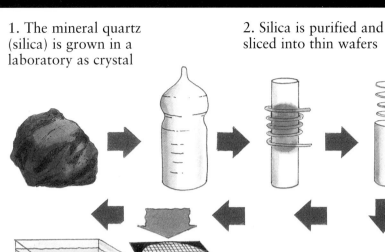

1. The mineral quartz (silica) is grown in a laboratory as crystal

2. Silica is purified and sliced into thin wafers

5. Acid removes coating to leave electronic circuit

4. Ultraviolet light burns in the circuits

3. Wafers are given a special coating

COMPUTER CRYSTALS

The mineral quartz (SiO_2) contains silicon and oxygen. It occurs in many forms in nature — including sand — and is a raw material for making glass. Quartz crystals are used in clocks, computers, and electronic equipment.

This enlarged view shows many microchips on a thin slice of the mineral silicon.

Crystals bend or deflect waves and rays, including light waves and X rays. This feature is used in the scientific laboratory test called X-ray crystallography.

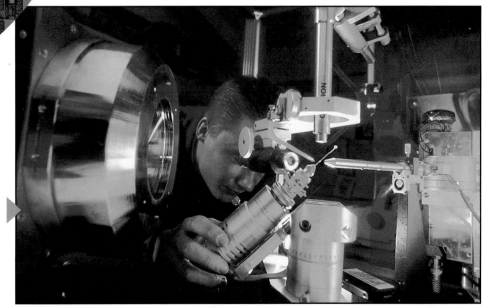

GEMSTONES AND JEWELS

Jewels are among the most precious objects in the world. They start as gemstones — raw mineral pieces that can sparkle, glow, or glint with beautiful colors when polished.

SIMPLE SUBSTANCES

Most jewels and gems, like diamonds, rubies, sapphires, and emeralds, are crystals of natural minerals. And most gems are made of simple chemical substances. Diamonds contains only carbon — the same substance that, in a different form, makes up soot. Rubies and sapphires are both crystals of the mineral corundum (Al_2O_3), which contains only aluminum and oxygen.

Gemstones are found only in a few types of rocks. The "Big Hole" is an inactive diamond mine near Kimberley, South Africa.

1. Diamond-containing kimberlite rock

2. Rock loosened, broken up, and loaded onto wagons

Most gemstones, like these rubies, are found in rocks as rough, dull-looking lumps. Only when cut and polished do they shine with great color.

14

Diamonds are used to make the teeth on some drill bits.

WHY SO PRECIOUS?

If jewels and gems contain only simple mineral substances, why are they so valuable? — partly because they are rare, making owning one a symbol of wealth and power. Most are also very hard and long-lasting — diamond is the hardest natural substance. And, of course, they can be cut and polished to shine and sparkle.

MINING AND PROCESSING DIAMONDS

Usually, a lump of rock bigger than a house must be crushed and sorted to find one small gemstone. In a typical diamond mine, the rock is loosened, broken up, crushed, ground, and mixed with water.

As the slurry is stirred, the heavier diamond-containing pieces sink and stick to a moving belt coated with thick grease. Jets of water wash away the remaining unwanted particles, leaving rough diamonds stuck in the grease.

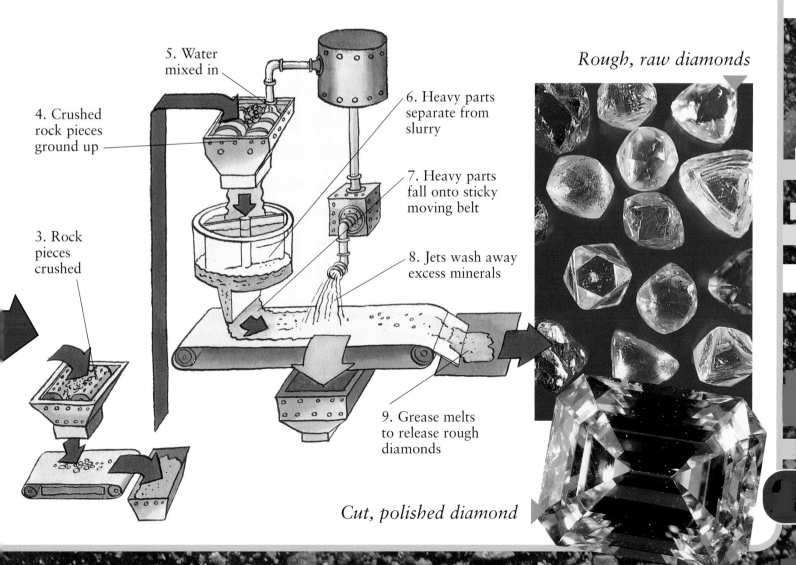

5. Water mixed in

4. Crushed rock pieces ground up

3. Rock pieces crushed

6. Heavy parts separate from slurry

7. Heavy parts fall onto sticky moving belt

8. Jets wash away excess minerals

9. Grease melts to release rough diamonds

Rough, raw diamonds

Cut, polished diamond

MINERALS FOR LIFE

Rocks and minerals are important not only for construction, factories, and industries. They are needed for the growth and health of crops, farm animals — and humans.

STAYING HEALTHY

The human body needs a regular supply of certain minerals to grow, stay healthy, and maintain strong bones and teeth. Usually there are plenty of these minerals in our food. But in some cases, tablets called supplements help supply minerals that may be missing from our diets.

Mineral fertilizers are first tested in the laboratory (left). If they are safe and do little harm to the environment, they can be made in bulk and spread on the land (above).

In some illnesses, the body cannot take in enough minerals from food. Mineral supplement tablets help boost supplies.

FACTS FROM THE PAST

Before fertilizers were made in factories, people used natural sources of minerals for their crops. One very rich source was guano, the huge piles of droppings from seabirds, bats, and other animals that live packed together in colonies. Mining guano was difficult and dangerous — and very smelly! Factory-made fertilizers began to take over in the 1920s.

Mining guano on an island off Peru, 1863

MAKING MINERAL-RICH FERTILIZER

Nitrates and phosphates are important minerals for plants. Phosphates come from crushed rocks. The raw materials of fertilizers are mixed in water-cooled tanks. The result is a soupy mix that is dried to a powder and put into bags.

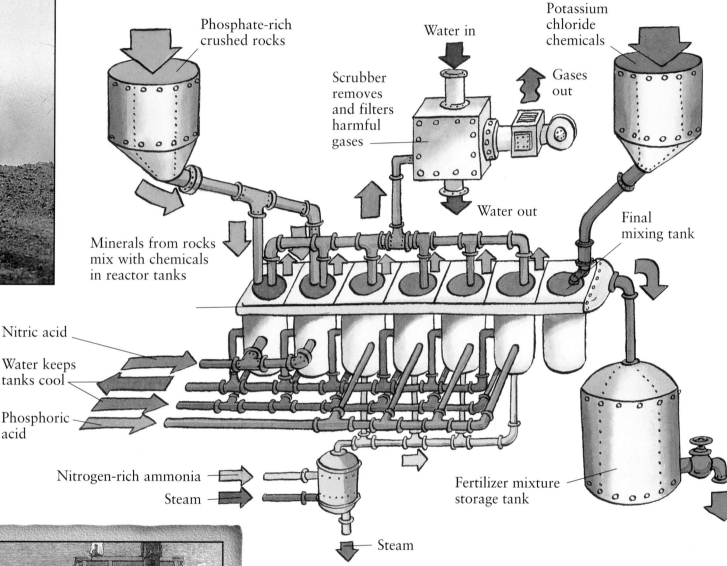

Phosphate-rich crushed rocks

Water in

Potassium chloride chemicals

Scrubber removes and filters harmful gases

Gases out

Water out

Final mixing tank

Minerals from rocks mix with chemicals in reactor tanks

Nitric acid

Water keeps tanks cool

Phosphoric acid

Nitrogen-rich ammonia

Steam

Fertilizer mixture storage tank

Steam

MINERALS ON THE FARM

Like people, farm animals such as sheep, cows, and pigs need regular supplies of minerals in their feed for healthy growth. Crops like wheat and rice require certain mixtures of minerals, too. These may occur naturally in the soil, but farmers can help crops grow by using mineral-rich fertilizers.

IN THE FUTURE

Will there be enough rocks and minerals to last into the future? Earth is so vast that there seems to be an endless supply of them. But one main problem is the way we mine, quarry, and process them.

THE NEED FOR ENERGY

Mines and quarries use huge machines with diesel engines or electric motors. These use up lots of energy. Also, cutting stone blocks, finding gems, baking ceramics, making cement, and processing fertilizers all require great amounts of energy. Supplies of oil, coal, and other energy fuels may run out long before rocks and minerals do.

Coal from mines (above) and oil from wells (left) are minerals that formed in Earth by natural processes long ago.

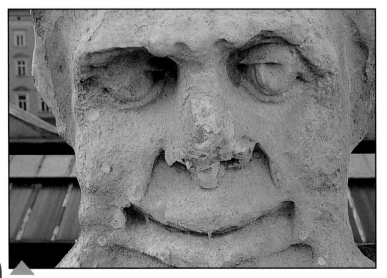

Acid-rain pollution damages even hard stone.

IDEAS FOR THE FUTURE

Could we obtain necessary minerals from other places in the Solar System? Perhaps. Six Apollo space missions visited the Moon from 1969 to 1972. They brought back almost 885 pounds (400 kilograms) of Moon rocks and dust. But the cost of the missions was so great that the Moon rocks were far more costly, for their weight, than the finest diamonds. Space mining is very unlikely in the foreseeable future.

28

Where rocks are plentiful on the ground, they can be built into environmentally friendly stone walls.

MAKING CRYSTALS

Many mines containing crystals and gems have already been "worked out." Although finding new sources is becoming difficult, some crystals can be made by machines. Ruby crystals are valuable for jewelry (*see page 24*) and in lasers and other high-tech equipment. They are a form of the mineral corundum, which is made up of aluminum and oxygen. Heat and high pressure are used to make these substances into rubies.

REUSE AND RECYCLING

There are many ways we can help save rocks, minerals, and energy for the future. Old building blocks and bricks can be cleaned and used again in new buildings, or they can be crushed and put into new building foundations. Valuable minerals and their products, such as ceramics, composites, and glass, can be recycled rather than thrown away.

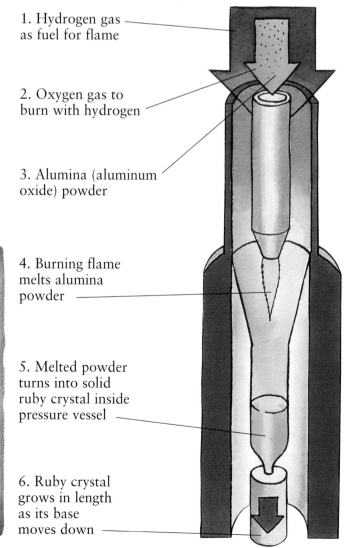

1. Hydrogen gas as fuel for flame

2. Oxygen gas to burn with hydrogen

3. Alumina (aluminum oxide) powder

4. Burning flame melts alumina powder

5. Melted powder turns into solid ruby crystal inside pressure vessel

6. Ruby crystal grows in length as its base moves down

Mining minerals in space — a distant dream?

ROCKS AND THEIR USES

TYPE OF ROCK		FEATURES AND USES
IGNEOUS	Granite	Very hard rock with large grains or crystals, usually in whites, grays, pinks, and yellows; used for building blocks and slabs
	Gabbro	Crumbly rock with large gray-green crystals; source of copper
	Basalt	Dark, small grains; crushed for road and railway foundations
	Obsidian	Hard, dark, glassy; used for jewelry, decorations and sculpture
	Pumice	Very light in weight and color, soft and crumbly, almost spongy; used to retain heat and as a soft abrasive
	Porphyry	Mixture of large pale and small dark grains; used for building
	Granophyre	Speckled pink, white, and black; used in decorative gravel paths
SEDIMENTARY	Chalk	Whitish, fairly soft, powdery form of limestone (*below*), made mainly of tiny fossils; used for drawing and marking
	Limestone	Varies greatly, usually white or pale with mixed grains and perhaps fossils; used for decorative slabs, walls, blocks, statues
	Flint	Colors vary from black to white, splits to give very sharp edges; used for making tools and weapons
	Tuff	Soft rock made of fine volcanic fragments; used for carving
	Dolomite	Light pink, gray, or yellow, with tiny grains or crystals, often contains oil (petroleum); used for building blocks
	Pudding stone	Large pebbles in fine gray powder; looks like concrete
METAMORPHIC	Mica schist	Multicolored streaks and lumps; used for bright decoration
	Gneiss	Mix of light and dark grains; used for building blocks and slabs
	Slate	Grayish, splits into thin sheets; used for roof tiles
	Marble	Beautiful streaks and swirls in many colors, easily shaped; used for statues, paving slabs, tiles, blocks, and decoration

bearing: a part of a machine that reduces friction to allow free movement between two moving parts.

chemical element: a pure substance, which cannot be broken up into any simpler substances. Oxygen, aluminum, and iron are all examples of chemical elements.

circuit: a closed path of parts that guides the flow of electricity inside a machine or electronic device, such as a computer.

composite: using parts from different sources.

environment: the surroundings, including water, air, soil, rocks, plants, and animals.

excavator: a large, mechanical shovel used in removing rock and soil from the ground.

fiber: a long, thin strand of natural or man-made material.

geologist: a scientist who studies rocks, minerals, the forces that shape the landscape, and Earth itself.

kiln: a large oven in which pottery or bricks are heated until they harden.

production line: a sequence of workers in a factory that make a product as it moves from one worker to the next.

seismic: related to a vibration or earthquake.

slurry: a thin mixture of a liquid and another substance, such as clay or cement, that cannot dissolve in the liquid.

MORE BOOKS TO READ

Crystal & Gem. Eyewitness series.
R. F. Symes (DK Publishing)

Dig It!: How to Collect Rocks and Minerals. Reader's Digest Explorer's Guides series.
Susan Tejada (Reader's Digest)

Minerals. Kaleidoscope: Earth Science series.
Roy A. Gallant (Benchmark Books)

Rocks & Minerals. Fantastic Facts series.
Jack Challoner (Southwater)

WEB SITES

Rock Hounds
http://sln.fi.edu/fellows/payton/rocks/index2.html

The Nature of Diamonds
http://www.amnh.org/exhibitions/diamonds

Due to the dynamic nature of the Internet, some web sites stay current longer than others. To find additional web sites, use a reliable search engine with one or more of the following keywords: *ceramic, clay, crystal, concrete, diamond, gemstone, geology, rock, microchip, mineral, quarry.*

INDEX